FROM

Other Helen Exley Giftbooks:
Love & Romance   Shakespeare on Love
To my very special Love

EDITED BY HELEN EXLEY
ILLUSTRATED BY JULIETTE CLARKE

Published simultaneously in 2000 by Exley Publications in
Great Britain, and Exley Publications LLC in the USA.
Copyright © Helen Exley 2000
The moral right of the author has been asserted.

12 11 10 9 8 7 6 5 4 3 2 1

ISBN 1-86187-166-X

Exley Publications Ltd, 16 Chalk Hill, Watford, Herts WD1 4BN, UK.
Exley Publications LLC, 232 Madison Avenue, Suite 1409,
NY 10016, USA.

Acknowledgements: The publishers are grateful for permission to reproduce
copyright material. Whilst every reasonable effort has been made to trace
copyright holders, the publishers would be pleased to hear from any not here
acknowledged. Tom McGrath: "Reasons" © Tom McGrath. Used by permission
of the author. Rosamunde Pilcher: From "The Stone Boy" © Rosamunde Pilcher
1983. Used by permission of Felicity Bryan on behalf of the author.

A LITTLE BOOK OF

Love

A HELEN EXLEY GIFTBOOK

NEW YORK • WATFORD, UK

Love is a wizard.... It intoxicates, it envelops, it isolates. It creates fragrance in the air, ardour from coldness, it beautifies everything around it.

LEOŠ JANÁČEK (1854–1928)

Love makes you everything you want to be.

STUART AND LINDA
MACFARLANE

Love... is so sweet —
Sweetest, dearest, fleetest comer,
Fledgling of the sudden summer.

LOUISE MOULTON

When Love speaks, the voice of
all the gods
Make heaven drowsy with
the harmony.

WILLIAM SHAKESPEARE
(1564-1616)

The greatest happiness
love can offer
is the first pressure
of hands between you
and your beloved.

STENDHAL (1783-1842)

The universe hangs
on a kiss, exists in the
hold of a kiss.

ZALMAN SHNEAR

The sweetest memory
of all is that first kiss
from your one true love.

STUART AND LINDA MACFARLANE

*Love is
huddling together
for shelter
under an umbrella —
long after the
rain has stopped.*

STUART AND LINDA MACFARLANE

Love should run
out to meet love
with open arms.

ROBERT LOUIS STEVENSON
(1850-1894)

*Love demands the
impossible, the
absolute, the sky on
fire, inexhaustible
springtime....*

ALBERT CAMUS (1913-1960)

ONE WORD FREES US

OF ALL THE WEIGHT

AND PAIN OF LIFE:

THAT WORD IS LOVE.

SOPHOCLES (496-406 B.C.)

Love feels no burden,
thinks nothing of trouble,
attempts what is above its
strength, pleads no excuse
of impossibility; for it
thinks all things lawful
for itself, and all things
possible.

THOMAS Á KEMPIS
(1379-1471)

LOVE COMMANDS US TO
STEP OUT INTO
NOTHINGNESS — AND
BEARS US UP.

PAM BROWN, b.1928

Love is the heart's
immortal thirst to be
completely known and
all forgiven.

HENRY VAN DYKE (1852-1933)

*... love means that
I am confident enough
about that other that I
can trust him with my gift.*

CAROL TRAVIS

What happiness to be beloved; and O, what bliss, ye gods, to love!

JOHANN WOLFGANG VON GOETHE
(1749-1832)

The supreme happiness of life is the conviction of being loved for yourself, or, more correctly, being loved in spite of yourself.

VICTOR HUGO (1802-1885)

You know how it is when it happens, like a search that's ended. And the wonderful relief at having found someone to go home and talk to, who knows you, understands your work and everything you're going through.

DERVLA KIRWAN, b.1971

Love makes
all hard
hearts gentle.

GEORGE HERBERT
(1583-1633)

Love is an act of endless forgiveness, a tender look which becomes a habit.

PETER USTINOV, b.1921

Love so amazing,
so divine
Demands my soul,
my life, my all.

ISAAC WATTS
(1674-1748)

MANY WATERS CANNOT QUENCH
LOVE, NEITHER CAN THE FLOODS
DROWN IT.

SONG OF SOLOMON

Love is... a flower so delicate
that a touch will bruise it,
so strong that nothing will
stop its growth.

FERN WHEELER

LOVE IS... A PARDONABLE INSANITY.

SÉBASTIEN CHAMFORT
(1741-1794)

Love is the triumph of
imagination over intelligence.

H.L. MENCKEN (1880-1956)

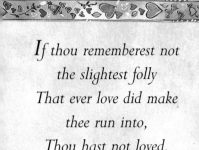

If thou rememberest not
the slightest folly
That ever love did make
thee run into,
Thou hast not loved.

WILLIAM SHAKESPEARE
(1564–1616)

PASSIONATE LOVE

Love isn't decent.
Love is glorious and shameless.

ELIZABETH VON ARNIM
(1866-1941)

Love is when the desire to be
desired takes you so badly that
you feel you could die of it.

HENRI DE TOULOUSE-LAUTREC
(1864-1901)

I LOVE THEE

TO THE DEPTH AND

BREADTH AND HEIGHT

MY SOUL CAN REACH....

ELIZABETH BARRETT BROWNING
(1806-1861)

All are my blooms, and all
sweet blooms of love
To thee I gave while spring
and summer sang.

ROSSETTI

Beauty is a light that shines through the most ordinary woman – if she is happy and in love.

PAM BROWN, b.1928

Scientists can write all the books they like about love being a trap of nature.... But all that scientists are going to convince are other scientists, not women in love.

AUTHOR UNKNOWN

In love. She remembered the excitement of those days. The sudden ecstasy of an unexpected telephone call. The brilliance and beauty of the most mundane objects. Laughter over nothing,

shared across small candlelit tables;
walking together on sunlit
pavements; smelling lilac on a city
street; driving in his car down to
the country, with the sun roof open
to the sky and a whole weekend
ahead, and the sensation that there
was nobody in the world but the
two of them.

ROSAMUNDE PILCHER, b.1924

Sweet one I love you
for your lovely shape,
for the art you make
in paint and bed and rhyme,
but most because we see
into each other's hearts,
there to read secrets
and to trust,
and cancel time.

TOM MCGRATH, b.1940

In Love With Her

... I see her every
day, and always
see her for the
first time.

JEAN RACINE
(1639-1699)

She is Venus when she smiles; but she's Juno when she walks; And Minerva when she talks.

BEN JONSON
(1572-1637)

Love is the strongest of nature's forces — able to bring joy even out of tragedy.

STUART AND LINDA MACFARLANE

A LOVER'S EYES WILL GAZE AN
EAGLE BLIND.
A LOVER'S EAR WILL HEAR THE
LOWEST SOUND.

WILLIAM SHAKESPEARE
(1564-1616)

Love is... born with the pleasure of looking at each other, it is fed with the necessity of seeing each other, it is concluded with the impossibility of separation!

JOSÉ MARTÍ (1853-1895)

Only love heals, makes whole, takes us beyond ourselves. Love... is both right motive and right result. Love gets us There....

MARSHA SINETAR

WHETHER RICH OR POOR,
WISE OR DULL, GOOD OR
BAD, WE ALL NEED AND
DESERVE LOVE.

STUART AND LINDA MACFARLANE

All, everything
that I understand,
I understand only
because I love.

LEO TOLSTOY (1828-1910)

I wonder why love is so often equated with joy when it is everything else as well. Devastation, balm, obsession, granting and receiving excessive value, and losing it again.

It is recognition, often of what you are not but might be. It sears and it heals. It is beyond pity and above law.

FLORIDA SCOTT-MAXWELL
(1883-1978)

My flocks feed not,
My ewes breed not,
My rams speed not,
All is amiss.
Love is dying,
Faith's defying,
Heart's denying,
Causer of this.

RICHARD BARNFIELD
(1574-1627)

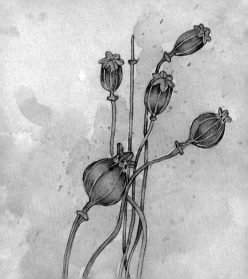

Ah! when will this long
weary day have end,
And lend me leave to
come unto my love?

EDMUND SPENCER

You may know the pains of possessing and dependency, reducing persons to objects, but this is not love. Love doesn't attempt to bind, ensnare, capture. It is light,

free of the burden
of attachments. Love
asks nothing, is
fulfilled in itself.
When love is there,
nothing remains to
be done.

VIMALA THAKAR

*Love takes
the bad with the good
and makes it all
very special.*

STUART AND LINDA MACFARLANE

*Familiar acts
are beautiful
through love.*

PERCY BYSSHE SHELLEY
(1792-1822)

True Love is but a humble,
low-born thing.
And hath its food served up
in earthen ware:

It is a thing to walk with,
hand in hand.
Through the everydayness of
this workday world.

JAMES RUSSELL LOWELL
(1819-1891)

I have drunk the wine of life
at last, I have known
the best thing best worth
knowing, I have been warmed
through and through, never
to grow quite cold again
till the end.

EDITH WHARTON (c.1861-1937),
ON FALLING IN LOVE AT AGE FORTY-SIX

LOVERS SLEEP IN UTTER
TRUST — RESIGNED TO
ONE ANOTHER WITH
THE CERTAINTY OF
CHILDHOOD — PASSION
TRANSFORMED TO
GENTLENESS, TO QUIET
CONTENT.

PAM BROWN, b.1928

Imparudis'd in one another's arms.

JOHN MILTON (1608-1674)

... their souls kissed,
they kissed with their eyes,
they were both but one
single kiss.

HEINRICH HEINE (1797-1856)

*Love does not consist
in gazing at each other
but in looking outward
together in the same direction.*

ANTOINE DE SAINT-EXUPÉRY
(1900-1944)

NOW OUR LOVE IS DEEP
ENOUGH TO NEED NO
FRANTIC GESTURES. YOU
SMILE IN PASSING, TOUCH MY
SHOULDER. I WALK WITH YOU
IN THE GARDEN, SHARING THE
LAST OF THE LIGHT, THE

FLICKERING OF BATS, THE
SCENT OF ROSES. WE ARE AT
HOME IN QUIETNESS. PASSION
AND THE EVERYDAY FLOW
FROM EACH OTHER, EQUAL
EXPRESSIONS OF OUR LOVE.

CHARLOTTE GRAY, b.1937

Keep love in your heart.
The consciousness of
loving and being loved
brings a warmth and
richness to life that
nothing else can bring.

OSCAR WILDE (1854-1900)

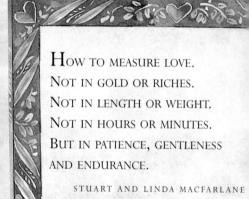

How to measure love.
Not in gold or riches.
Not in length or weight.
Not in hours or minutes.
But in patience, gentleness
and endurance.

STUART AND LINDA MACFARLANE

*Love has nothing to
do with what you are
expecting to get — only
what you are expecting to
give — which is everything.*

KATHARINE HEPBURN, b.1909

Love must be learned,
and learned again and again;
there is no end to it.

KATHERINE ANNE PORTER
(1890-1980)

Love is enriched by every
good thing shared — and
made stronger by every sorrow
faced together.

PAM BROWN, b.1928

BUILDING TOGETHER

Love doesn't just
sit there, like a
stone; it has to be
made, like bread,
remade all the time,
made new.

URSULA K. LE GUIN, b.1929

Love consists in
desiring to give
what is our own to
another and feeling
his delight as our
own.

EMANUEL SWEDENBORG
(1688-1772)

Love suffers long and is kind; love does not envy; love does not parade itself, is not puffed up; does not behave rudely, does not seek its own, is not provoked, thinks no evil; does not rejoice in iniquity, but rejoices in the truth; bears all things, believes all things, hopes all things, endures all things. Love never fails.

1 CORINTHIANS 13:4-8

Love is a plant of tenderest growth: treat it well, take thought for it and it may grow strong and perfume your whole life.

FRANK HARRIS (1856-195[1])

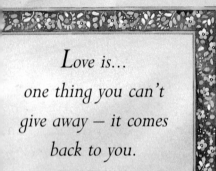

Love is...

one thing you can't

give away — it comes

back to you.

TRADITIONAL

*T*hose who love deeply
never grow old;
they may die of old age,
but they die young.

SIR ARTHUR WING PINERO
(1855-1934)

LOVE BETWEEN THE
VERY YOUNG IS TOUCHING.
LOVE BETWEEN THE
VERY OLD IS GLORY.

PAM BROWN, b.1928

Memories

One does not remember the
flowers or the compliments.
One remembers standing at an
upstairs window staring down the
evening-shadowed street waiting
for him to turn the corner.

Love knows no limits to its endurance, no end to its trust, no dashing of its hope; it can outlast anything. It is, in fact the one thing that still stands when all else has fallen.

1 CORINTHIANS 13:1-2, 4-7

LOVE... WIPES OUT ALL SENSE OF TIME,
DESTROYING ALL MEMORY OF A
BEGINNING AND ALL FEAR OF AN END.

MADAME DE STAËL
(1766-1817)

There is only one terminal
dignity – love.... It is perhaps
the only glimpse we are
permitted of eternity.

HELEN HAYES, b.1900

Love – the most
permanent of
human emotions.

STUART AND LINDA MACFARLANE

Love is something
eternal – the aspect
may change, but not
the essence.

VINCENT VAN GOGH (1853-1890)

Common as
light is love,
And its familiar
voice wearies
not ever.

PERCY BYSSHE SHELLEY
(1792-1822)

Is it so small a thing
To have enjoyed the sun,
To have lived light in the spring,
To have loved, to have thought,
to have done?

MATTHEW ARNOLD (1822-1888)

No never forget!...
Never forget any
moment;
they are too few.

ELIZABETH BOWEN
(1899-1973)